Contents

A sneaky cat

A Bengal tiger spots a deer in the rainforest. The tiger slinks through the trees and tall grass. It stays silent as it creeps up on its prey. Then the tiger leaps on to the deer.

A Bengal tiger has black, orange and white fur. The colours help it to blend in with the rising and setting sun. Those are the times tigers hunt most often. Their black stripes look like shadows from a distance. Deer, antelope and wild pigs don't see a tiger until it's too late.

A Bengal tiger's body

Tigers belong to a group of animals called big cats. Lions and jaguars are also in this group. Tigers are the largest of the big cats. Adult Bengal tigers can weigh up to about 227 kilograms (500 pounds). They are almost 3 metres (10 feet) long. Only the Siberian tiger is bigger than the Bengal.

Bengal tigers have strong legs and shoulders. Their back legs are longer than their front legs. Bengals push off their back legs to jump on to prey.

Their large, yellow eyes help Bengal tigers find prey easily. Tigers can see well, even at night. Their eyes have a special layer that lets in more light. The extra light helps tigers to see well in the dark. At night their eyes glow when light hits this layer.

Whiskers grow on the Bengal's face
and body. They help the tiger to move
around in the dark to find food.

Roar! Bengal tigers bite prey with their four canine teeth. These sharp teeth can break bone. The tiger's back teeth help it to tear meat from the bone.

Bengals have four large, padded paws. The pads let them move quietly when following prey.

Long, sharp claws grow from
the Bengal tiger's paws. Tigers use
their claws to slash and hold prey.
When it's not hunting, the tiger
pulls the claws into its paws.

Life in the forest

Wild Bengal tigers live mainly in India. They are sometimes called Indian tigers. About half of all wild tigers are Bengal tigers. Bengals live in rainforests and grasslands.

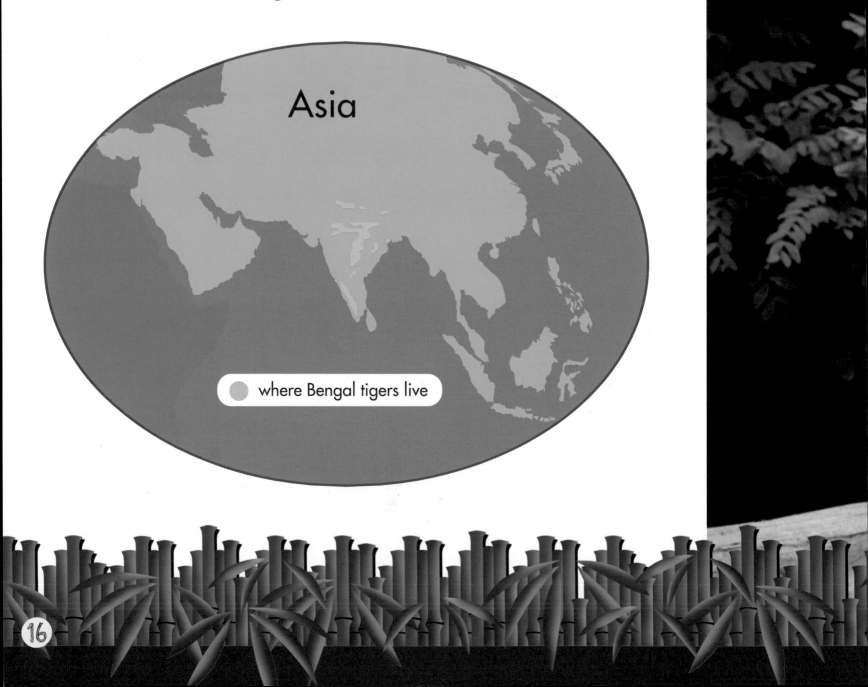

Asia

where Bengal tigers live

Bengal tigers live alone, except when mothers are raising their young. Each adult has its own home area called a range. Bengals scrape the ground and trees to mark their range. A pile of tiger poo tells other tigers to keep out.

Bengal tigers roar to keep other tigers away. Males also roar at females when it's time to mate. A Bengal tiger's roar can be heard up to 3 kilometres (2 miles) away!

Splash! Bengal tigers often live near water. They swim to cool off. They even chase prey into lakes and streams. Tigers are more at home in water than other big cats.

Bengal tigers sleep during the day. They hunt for food at night. Tigers usually hunt alone.

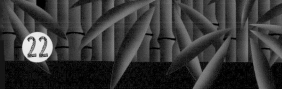

Bengal tigers eat about once or twice a week. Sometimes a Bengal can't finish a meal. It hides food in tall grass for later.

Growing up

Female Bengals give birth to a litter of cubs about three months after mating. Most litters have two or three cubs. Newborns weigh about 1.4 kilograms (3 pounds). They can't see and have fuzzy fur.

Let's play! Bengal tiger cubs learn how to hunt by playing. They chase and jump on each other. They even pounce on their mothers. Females teach their cubs how to hunt.

Cubs stay with their mothers for about two years. In the wild, Bengal tigers can live for up to 15 years.

Saving Bengal tigers

Today all tigers are endangered. Fewer than 2,000 Bengal tigers remain in the wild. Tigers lose their homes when forests are cut down. Humans poach Bengals too.

In India, land is set aside for Bengal tigers to live on. Zoos also breed Bengals. People work together to save these awesome Asian animals.

Glossary

breed mate and produce young

canine long, pointed tooth

cub young animal such as a tiger, cheetah, polar bear or lion

endangered in danger of dying out

grassland large, open area where grass and low plants grow

litter group of animals born at the same time to the same mother

mate join together to produce young

poach take animals or fish illegally

prey animal hunted by another animal for food

rainforest thick forest where a great deal of rain falls

range area where an animal mainly lives

shadow dark shape made by something blocking out light

Books

All About Tigers (Text Structures: Description Text),
Philip Simpson (Raintree, 2014)

Animals in Danger in Asia, Richard and Louise Spilsbury
(Raintree, 2013)

Tigers (Usborne Beginners), James Maclaine (Usborne
Publishing Ltd, 2012)

Websites

www.bbc.co.uk/nature/life/Tiger/
Find out interesting facts about tigers, and go on a tiger quest.

http://gowild.wwf.org.uk/asia
Learn fun facts, read stories and make tiger crafts.

www.ngkids.co.uk/did-you-know/10-tiger-facts
Are tigers the largest wild cats? Find this answer and more!

Comprehension questions

1. Bengal tigers belong to a group of animals called big cats.
   Name two other animals that belong to this group.

2. How does the colour of the Bengal tiger's fur help it to hunt
   for prey?

3. Bengal tigers are endangered. What does "endangered" mean?

Index